CAREERS

essential careers™

CAREERS IN
SECURITY

JERI FREEDMAN

ROSEN
PUBLISHING®

NEW YORK

Published in 2014 by The Rosen Publishing Group, Inc.
29 East 21st Street, New York, NY 10010

First Edition

Library of Congress Cataloging-in-Publication Data

Freedman, Jeri.
Careers in security/Jeri Freedman.—1st ed.
     p. cm.—(Essential careers)
Includes bibliographical references and index.
ISBN 978-1-4488-9474-1 (library binding)
1. Private security services—Vocational guidance—United States. 2. Security consultants—United States. I. Title.
HV8291.U6F74 2014
363.28'902373
                                                                    2012040035

Manufactured in the United States of America

CPSIA Compliance Information: Batch #S13YA: For further information, contact Rosen Publishing, New York, New York, at 1-800-237-9932.

contents

With huge crowds and millions of dollars of property and merchandise to protect, mall security guards have a large responsibility in keeping people, premises, and valuables safe.

DUCTION

U nfortunately, safety, crime, and terrorism are issues that people have to deal with. Individuals and property are often in danger, and the likelihood of crime and violence can increase when the economy is depressed. For this reason, there is a high demand for personnel in all types of security jobs, and the security field offers a wide range of jobs that can provide reliable employment in both good times and times of economic uncertainty. A career in security can provide the satisfaction of knowing that one is helping and protecting people. Many jobs in this field can also be interesting and exciting.

Security jobs exist in private companies, at public venues such as sports facilities and arenas, and in government agencies. One of the appealing aspects of the security field is that it provides jobs that offer dependable salaries and good benefits for people with all levels of education. Jobs range from security guards and government security agents at airports to college-educated government agents and intelligence analysts. The field also includes a wide variety of working environments—from one-person operations to huge corporations, and from celebrity protection to corporate security to agencies involved in international crime and terrorism prevention.

The security field is likely to remain strong for many years to come. A job in the security industry can also provide opportunities for career advancement. Many people who start out in entry-level jobs move on to supervisory or management positions. Also, many companies in the field reimburse employees for courses taken to gain additional skills or degrees. Thus, the security area provides a steady, often interesting job, with good benefits, that also has the potential for advancement in the field.

chapter 1

THE SECURITY FIELD

The security field consists of organizations and individuals responsible for the protection of people and property, both physical and virtual. Because of the wide range of services provided in this area, it offers jobs for people with all levels of education and different physical and technical skills. There are two main sectors within the security industry: the public (government) sector and the private sector. Some activities of security professionals are common to both sectors, whereas others are limited to the public sector.

THE SECURITY INDUSTRY

Some aspects of security include physical security, personal security, cybersecurity, loss prevention and risk management, emergency preparedness, crime prevention and investigation, counterterrorism, and disaster management. Physical security involves making sure that criminals, terrorists, employees, and visitors do not damage, destroy, or steal property or facilities. Personal security is the protection of individuals on both a collective and individual basis. Loss prevention and risk management require putting in place systems to protect against the loss of property, as well as ensuring that the company complies with local, state, and federal regulations so that it is not liable for harm that befalls employees or visitors. Emergency preparedness involves developing plans to deal with human-made and natural disasters, and disaster management involves putting those plans into action and working with local, state, or federal authorities to protect people and property during a disaster and subsequent recovery. Crime prevention and investigation require identifying potential threats, and collecting and interpreting evidence to identify those who commit crimes. Cybersecurity is the prevention of theft of information and data stored on computers. Counterterrorism is the protection of people and property from terrorist attacks and is most commonly carried out by government agencies.

Jobs in the security industry range from first responders—those who are first on the scene to deal with a crime or disaster—to intelligence analysts who work behind the scenes to analyze information that may lead to the arrest of a criminal

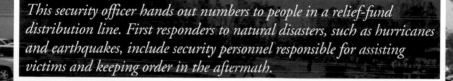

This security officer hands out numbers to people in a relief-fund distribution line. First responders to natural disasters, such as hurricanes and earthquakes, include security personnel responsible for assisting victims and keeping order in the aftermath.

or terrorist. The field offers a variety of job situations to suit different people. One can work for a large corporation, entertainment venue, small or large private security firm, private detective organization, or government agency. The advantages of working in a large firm or government agency are good benefits and salaries, and, in many positions, predictable hours. At higher levels, a professional may be on call to deal with emergencies at times when regular employees are off the clock. Also, such jobs are often high pressure, with the responsibility for dealing with major problems. In the case of lower-level employees, job advancement may be limited.

Working for a private security firm may provide the opportunity to work in a variety of companies and roles, which can keep the job interesting. However, depending on the size of the firm, salaries and benefits may not be as good as at a corporation or government agency. Also, the schedule may be unpredictable. So, when choosing a career in the security field, it is important for a person to first consider what he or she wants from a job. He or she will then be in a better position to decide what type of organization and area of security will suit his or her personality and goals best.

PRIVATE SECURITY

The private security industry protects companies' and organizations' buildings and property, as well as their employees and visitors. Those who work in this sector of the security industry are also responsible for protecting the intellectual property and information of companies and organizations. Intellectual property refers to ideas and inventions that are developed by individuals and companies. Intellectual property includes patents and copyrights for products and creative works, such as books and movies. Private security professionals also protect a

The Outlook for the Security Industry

Worldwide security is one of the fastest-growing career fields. According to the *Occupational Outlook Handbook* published by the U.S. Bureau of Labor Statistics (also available online at http://www.bls.gov/ooh), employment for security guards is expected to grow 18 percent between 2010 and 2020. Jobs in security management, involving the analysis of and planning for security needs, is expected to grow by a similar amount. The increase is being driven by rising concern with crime, vandalism, and terrorism. The demand for information security analysts, who work in the area of cybersecurity, is expected to intensify by 22 percent. The demand for private detectives is expected to climb 21 percent over the same period because of the increased need to protect both confidential information and products. The need for forensic technicians, who collect and analyze physical evidence, is expected to grow by 19 percent. However, competition for forensic jobs is keen because interest in the field has been increased by popular television shows. As you can see from these growth rates, security is likely to remain a healthy area of employment for at least the next decade.

company's data and information from being stolen. Security professionals in private institutions such as art museums screen visitors and carry out pre-employment screening of potential employees. They investigate problems such as theft of company property. They also work with local and state law enforcement personnel in cases of crime or natural disasters that affect the company, among other functions. Private security firms

Institutions such as museums employ security personnel to ensure the safety of the art and artifacts they house. These precious items need to be protected from damage as well as theft.

perform such services for companies and institutions on a contract or as-needed basis. They also provide monitoring of private residences, working with law enforcement in case of break-ins and emergencies.

One of the largest career areas in the private sector is that of security guard. Most medium-sized to large companies hire security guards to protect their premises and screen visitors. So do institutions such as hospitals, educational facilities, and facilities open to the public, such as museums, sports arenas, and shopping centers. Security guards are employed by banks and financial institutions, and others are employed at apartment complexes. Roughly half the security guard positions in the United States are in private security firms and armored car services.

Employees of the Transportation Security Administration are responsible for checking passengers and baggage at transportation facilities such as airports to make certain that people can travel without danger.

PUBLIC SECURITY

In the post–9/11 era, there has been a vast increase in the number of security personnel employed by the government. The U.S. Secret Service is one employer of security personnel. The Department of Homeland Security employs border patrol agents to control drug trafficking and the passage of illegal aliens as well as personnel to identify and stop potential threats to the United States. The Transportation Security Administration (TSA) employs the people who handle security at transportation venues such as airports and train stations. Immigration and Customs agents provide security to control the passage of illegal goods into the United States and ensure that people who may be dangerous do not enter the country. Working for the government provides a steady income and excellent benefits, such as health insurance. The disadvantages include vulnerability to layoffs due to cutbacks in government spending and the fact that salaries in some positions are lower than in the private sector. Depending on the type of position, many security jobs involve significant personal danger. This is especially true in certain front-line government security jobs.

chapter 2

PROVIDING PRIVATE SECURITY

The information here describes in detail the day-to-day activities of security personnel in the private sector. These activities vary widely, depending on the specific type of job. Also covered are the career paths that various jobs in private security can provide.

CORPORATE SECURITY

Companies of all sizes need to protect their property, employees, and data. Security personnel in companies are responsible for detecting and stopping theft, workplace violence, industrial espionage, computer hacking, and white-collar crime such as fraud. Security jobs at companies range from security guard to director of security. Those in corporate security must be able to detect crimes, stop those committing crimes or engaging in violence on the job, and develop plans to keep such incidents from happening again in the future. In addition to dealing with crimes and violence, corporate security personnel are often called on to deal with accidents because they have experience handling emergencies and emergency services, such as ambulance companies and law enforcement agencies. Security personnel tackle sensitive legal areas. To protect the company

One responsibility of corporate security personnel is to control the access of visitors to the company's property, and they must make sure that visitors only have access to appropriate areas.

from being sued, they must be familiar with the laws and regulations that govern taking charge of suspects. They must also
understand the proper measures to take when dealing with visitors and employees on the company's premises. It is up to the
security manager or director to make sure that the company
complies with all regulations regarding security, such as ade-
quate lighting around the premises and maintenance of
emergency equipment.

It is important to be aware that private security personnel,
despite the fact that they wear uniforms and might carry weapons, are not police. They must respect the rights of the people
in their place of work according to the law and are not empow-
ered to make arrests. Corporate security professionals generally
develop close relationships with their local police force so that
they can call on law enforcement professionals to assist them
when they detect a crime.

Large companies and facilities may employ many people
at various levels in the security department. At the entry
level, security staff may check visitor and employee IDs,
inspect the premises to make sure they are secure, and keep
track of people's activities on monitors. At the highest levels, the security professional will spend most of his or her
time in management activities. These include drawing up
plans for emergency response, reviewing reports and activities of lower-level employees to detect signs of problems,
and presenting reports and recommendations to company
management. In addition, security managers and directors
are responsible for general managerial duties. They must
develop and monitor a departmental budget, hire and fire
personnel, and review and approve proposed purchases of
equipment, supplies, and services. Private security professionals may work at business premises, warehouses,
apartment buildings, utilities, mines, health facilities,
schools, or construction sites, among other locations.

TIPS ON GETTING A JOB IN CYBERSECURITY

Brian Duckering is a senior manager of Symantec's Endpoint Management and Mobility group. In an *InformationWeek* magazine article by Cindy Walker, "Four Tips: How to Land an IT Security Job," he had these suggestions for those interested in getting a cybersecurity job:

- *Consider certification:* In a competitive job market, certifications have increased in value.
- *Go back to school:* "An MBA in information systems, for example, can teach future security executives about data communications and systems analysis, as well as the impact security breaches can have in the areas of finance, marketing, and accounting."
- *Delve into mobile:* Mobile is one of the fastest-growing areas of computer systems, and understanding how to provide security for it is a skill in demand.
- *Mingle:* "Sometimes the quickest way to learn about what it takes to become a security professional is simply to spend time with one. 'Find a friend who's an IT security professional. Go to developer conferences. Get in with security people. . . . Ask them how they're making sure their data is secure. Pester them with questions.'"

CYBERSECURITY

Cybersecurity is an area that has become increasingly important since the 1990s. "Cyber" means "computer." In the twenty-first century, companies store massive amounts of valuable information on computer systems. Protecting a company's digital data and information from being stolen is called cybersecurity. Types of data include original research, specifications for new products being developed, lists of customers and clients, credit card and personal information of customers, and financial information on the company, among others. Protecting a company's property and data often requires security personal to staff and maintain use of security systems. A security system might include any combination of video cameras, alarms, electronic (card key) locks, and other devices. These systems are controlled by a computer with special programs.

A career in cybersecurity requires training in information technology as well as security techniques. Individuals in this

People with computer training and experience are in high demand in the security field to maintain and run computerized security systems, which are key to modern security efforts.

area must know how to use computer hardware and software to detect outsiders, hackers, and unauthorized users and deny them access to the company's computer systems. Cybersecurity

THE CHALLENGES OF WORKING IN PRIVATE SECURITY

Working in private security can be interesting, challenging, fulfilling, and at times exciting. However, there are a number of challenges that professionals face in private security. Foremost among them is the personal danger experienced by those who work in this field. There is always the risk that criminals or terrorists will turn violent and cause injury or even death to those who have to confront them. In addition, security professionals are usually first responders, those who are first on the scene when a crime or natural disaster occurs, facing danger from debris, fumes, and treacherous rubble.

In addition to physical danger, security positions can be stressful because responsibility for people's lives falls on the shoulders of the security managers and staff. At the same time, security professionals must be aware of the laws and regulations that cover what they can and cannot do in the course of their jobs. If they overstep the bounds of what is legal, they may open themselves up to lawsuits by people who feel they were mistreated.

Many security jobs also require continual practice and testing in areas such as firearms and detection techniques. Therefore, it is necessary to constantly maintain and update one's skills. Of course, physical condition is of prime importance in ensuring the safety of both the security professional and the people he or she protects. Thus, being a security professional requires a serious commitment to keeping one's body in shape and one's physical skills sharp.

professionals must also train employees to detect attempts to obtain their passwords and enforce rules that make employee passwords hard to guess. In addition, they must make sure that backup copies of the company's data and information are stored at a secure off-site facility so that they can be restored in case of a human-made or natural disaster that destroys the company's computers.

SPORTS AND ENTERTAINMENT SECURITY

All types of sports complexes, theaters, and arenas employ security professionals. Some security staff are employed by the facility at which sports or shows are presented. Others work for security firms that provide contract labor for special events. Security professionals at public venues are responsible for the same activities as those who work at corporations. However, they may also have to be versed in dealing with terrorism. They must ensure that visitors and participants are screened for weapons, recognize the signs of dangerous activity, and have a plan for protecting visitors and participants in the event of trouble.

Those who work in venues where large numbers of people congregate must draw up and implement plans that protect visitors and participants. Risk management is an area of facilities management that deals with reducing the chances of a crisis occurring during a sporting or entertainment event. The security manager must draw up a plan that identifies potential threats and vulnerabilities in the facility and describes how to deal with emergencies. Such a plan would identify who should respond and which emergency services and law enforcement agencies will be contacted. It also includes the way that spectators and participants will be evacuated from the facility, if necessary. If an emergency occurs, the security team is

Security professionals at sporting facilities must identify dangerous individuals and stop them before they can harm spectators and others, a challenging task because of the large numbers of people attending events.

responsible for controlling the situation and keeping fans, employees, and participants safe.

CRIMINAL INVESTIGATION JOBS

A unique profession in private-sector security is that of private detective. Private detectives are employed by individuals and companies for a range of purposes. A company might employ a detective to investigate ongoing theft of material, for example. Detectives are also employed by private individuals in order to uncover information about another person's activities or to locate a missing person or property. They may also carry out investigations for lawyers whose clients are involved in lawsuits or in criminal cases. Private investigators must learn how to trace people both electronically and through records, and interview people. They must also learn to follow people without being observed, detect lies, and defend themselves, among other skills.

A private detective works in his office, where he has to perform research involving both paper and electronic documents to find information of use in solving his cases.

Some of the common activities that private investigators engage in include the following: performing background

WORKING AS A BOUNTY HUNTER

One career that is related to security and seems exciting is that of bounty hunter. Bounty hunters track down and bring back fugitives. Fugitives are people who have run away after being charged with a crime. Bounty hunters earn a living by being paid for the return of the fugitive. When a criminal is arrested, he or she can sometimes remain free while awaiting trial by posting a certain amount of money, called bail. Often the amount is more than the accused person has. In that case, he or she can get a loan from a bail bondsman. If the person runs off—skips bail—the bail bondsman may offer to pay a bounty hunter to track the person down and bring him or her back. The payment is usually a percentage of the amount of bail. Some bounty hunters also work as skiptracers, people who track the whereabouts of individuals by electronic and other means but do not catch and bring back the person in question. Skiptracing is often performed for debt-collecting and other purposes not related to crime.

Bounty hunters can enter the property of fugitives to re-arrest them but cannot enter other people's property. Some states have training and licensing requirements for bounty hunters, whereas others don't require licensing, just that the bounty hunter operate under the control of a bail bondsman. However, when crossing state lines, a bounty hunter may work in the new state only if he or she is licensed there—or not at all if the state prohibits bounty hunting. In addition, bounty hunters are generally prohibited from pursuing fugitives to other countries. Successful bounty hunters can earn a significant amount of money. However, bounty hunting can be extremely dangerous because one is often dealing with violent and armed criminals. Being a bounty hunter requires great organizing, survival, and physical skills. In addition, because they are not law enforcement personnel, bounty hunters do not have the legal protections given to the police, and they can get into trouble if they kill a fugitive or injure nonfugitives.

checks on prospective employees, investigating claims of theft for insurance companies, and checking information submitted for credit applications and insurance policies. At times they are hired to go undercover at a company to investigate cases of theft or sabotage. In many locales, private investigators must be licensed. Licensing requirements vary by state. A typical example from Massachusetts includes these requirements: filling out an application, certification by three individuals in the locale where the applicant will practice that he or she is of good character, and three years of experience working for another private investigator, unless the applicant has previous law enforcement experience. The applicant cannot have been convicted of a felony (a serious crime). Many private investigators work for private detective agencies that employ multiple detectives. Others work independently on a freelance basis or are employed as store or hotel detectives to prevent illegal activities on those premises.

WORKING FOR A SECURITY FIRM

Although many security professionals work directly for one corporation or organization, a great many are employed for firms that provide contract security services. These firms provide services such as alarm monitoring and bodyguard services, as well as on-site contract security guards. Private security firms may specialize in certain areas like celebrity protection or guarding the valuable assets of museums. Other firms provide transportation of money and valuables via armored car. Some private security firms work internationally, providing security for U.S. companies overseas. One example is the security of the facilities of U.S. contractors employed for the U.S. government in Iraq and

Security agents safeguard Lady Gaga while she visits a community. Celebrity security includes protecting the celebrity from deliberate or accidental harm that might occur when he or she is in public. Large crowds around a performance venue often can provide a challenge.

Afghanistan. Working for a security company provides one with a steady salary and benefits, as well as the opportunity to perform various types of duties in different locations. The degree of danger involved varies greatly, depending on the type of security involved. Bodyguards and those working overseas in perilous places face potentially life-threatening hazards.

chapter 3

Working in Government Security

The day-to-day responsibilities and activities of personnel involved in the different areas of public-sector security are discussed here. Many of the government security jobs in the United States fall under the Department of Homeland Security (DHS). The DHS is charged with protecting the nation's infrastructure and people from criminals, terrorists, and natural disasters, and with planning for a prompt and effective response in the event of disaster.

U.S. Federal Security Services

A number of federal agencies employ security personnel and security support staff. The major security agencies offer a variety of employment opportunities.

The U.S. Secret Service

The official mission of the U.S. Secret Service is "to safeguard the nation's financial infrastructure and payment systems to preserve the integrity of the economy, and to protect national leaders, visiting heads of state and government, designated sites and National Special Security Events (NSSEs)." When most people think of the Secret Service, they think of the agents who protect the president of the United States. However, protecting the president and other dignitaries is only one aspect of the Secret Service. It protects important national sites and provides security for important government events. It also protects the U.S. financial structure, including the banking system and currency, by fighting counterfeiting, financial crimes, and electronic crimes. To do this it uses high-tech scientific and electronic technology, and trains agents in investigative techniques. It works with state, local, and international law enforcement agencies in fighting these crimes. In addition to field agents, who perform protective and investigative functions, it employs people with scientific and computer skills. These people collect, monitor, and analyze information. Information technology staff are also required to maintain and

U.S. Secret Service agents surround President Barack Obama at an international airport. Secret Service agents are responsible for protecting the president and his family. They must be prepared to risk their own lives to defend the president.

support the agency's computer systems. The Secret Service also employs administrators and support personnel, as in any large organization. Thus, it provides employment for people with a large range of skills.

The Secret Service has high standards for those it employs. To be a field agent, applicants must have a four-year college degree or a combination of education and previous criminal justice experience, be in good physical condition, and have no record of criminal behavior. Field agent work can be demanding and dangerous.

THE FEDERAL BUREAU OF INVESTIGATION

The Federal Bureau of Investigation (FBI) is responsible for gathering information on and dealing with threats within the borders of the United States. The FBI investigates crimes relating to terrorism, spying, cybercrime, public corruption, organized crime, violation of civil rights, and fraud. It also investigates a variety of major

The FBI *employs people with technical skills to maintain* its *comput-erized databases of information, which are* used to *identify suspects and analyze evidence.*

crimes such as art theft and bank robbery. According to the FBI Web site (http://www.fbi.gov), as of 2012, the FBI employed 35,951 people. That total included 13,897 special agents and 22,054 support professionals, such as intelligence analysts, language specialists, scientists, information technology specialists, and other professionals. FBI staff work at facilities in major U.S. cities and at local and regional offices in smaller cities and towns. They also work at more than sixty offices, called "legal attachés," located at U.S. embassies around the world. Like the Secret Service, the FBI employs front-line agents who investigate terrorism, espionage, and crime, and apprehend criminals.

THE CENTRAL INTELLIGENCE AGENCY

The Central Intelligence Agency (CIA) is responsible for gathering information about and responding to foreign threats. It collects information on foreign governments, agents, and terrorists. The CIA's Clandestine Service employs agents who live and work overseas gathering foreign intelligence and carrying out particular missions. Those in these positions spend 60 to 70 percent of their careers overseas. In addition to field agents, the service employs operations officers, information collection officers, and staff officers who manage the activities of the agents in the field. In addition to Clandestine Service positions, the CIA employs analysts who evaluate data and information, translators, and business and information technology personnel. In addition, it employs scientists in chemistry, biology, physics, and engineering who perform technical research and development.

THE NATIONAL SECURITY AGENCY

The National Security Agency (NSA) is responsible for collecting and analyzing data and information from both international and domestic sources. It looks for patterns that could indicate activity on the part of spies, terrorists, or other entities that are a threat to the United States. The NSA employs staff in the areas of languages, intelligence gathering, engineering, security investigation, and all areas of computer science and technology.

THE TRANSPORTATION SECURITY ADMINIS-TRATION

The Transportation Security Administration is a division of the DHS. Its mission is to protect U.S. transportation systems and ensure the safe passage of people and goods. It employs fifty thousand security officers, inspectors, air marshals, directors, and managers. They perform inspections and patrol airports, subways, and the railways. The TSA employs transportation

Border Patrol agents search a person apprehended while trying to enter the United States illegally. Stopping people from entering illegally includes identifying known or suspected terrorists and criminals.

security officers, border patrol agents, security administrators, asylum officers, contact representatives, criminal investigators, intelligence operations specialists, and airport security officers. It also employs program management specialists and general administrative staff.

INTERVIEW WITH A MEMBER OF THE TSA

Maria is a TSA security officer at a major U.S. airport, who consented to be interviewed.

What is your job and what do you do in it?

I am a security officer. The objective of my job is to ensure that passengers at airports travel safely. I check passengers' IDs and boarding passes to make sure they are valid and right. I also give them advisories on how to follow travel regulations related to their property and personal belongings. I examine passengers' property, bags, shoes, etc., when they have been stopped for carrying prohibited items, in order to confiscate them or give passengers alternatives for what to do with them. I search and pat down passengers manually who have been stopped at the walk-through metal detector or who require it due to different personal disabilities.

How did you become a security officer?

I applied for my job at a job fair, but I could have done it at the Web site www.tsa.gov by clicking on "jobs." I had to take an English test, an image test, and go through a background criminal investigation. When I was approved after three months, I was scheduled to have a week's training before entering the airport.

Once at the airport, I went through an on-the-job-training (OJT) period of about two months. At the end of my OJT, I had to take an imagery test in order to become an officer officially and work by myself.

What education and skills are needed for the job?

You must finish high school and be able to communicate orally and in writing in English. You must pass an imagery test (being able to detect threats and prohibited items in a variety of bags).

IMMIGRATION AND CUSTOMS CAREERS

The U.S. Immigration and Customs Enforcement (ICE) service is the primary investigative and enforcement arm of the DHS. It was created in 2003 by merging the security elements of the U.S. Immigration and Naturalization Service and the U.S. Customs Service. It is responsible for the enforcement of laws relating to the passage of goods and people into the United States. It has twenty thousand employees in all fifty states as well as forty-seven foreign countries. It has two main divisions: Homeland Security Investigations (HSI) and Enforcement and Removal Operations. ICE is responsible for ensuring that illegal goods and people who are a threat to U.S. security do not get into the country. It is also responsible for finding illegal immigrants and deporting them. Doing so requires carrying out an investigation, arresting and detaining suspects, and going through the legal process to send them back to the country they came from.

ICE employs security personnel at all levels. Special agents are responsible for carrying out investigations. Border patrol agents protect the U.S. borders. Customs agents examine and control goods and people entering the United States.

Immigration and Customs Enforcement agents are responsible for finding and arresting people who are trying to smuggle dangerous goods such as guns, drugs, or weapons of mass destruction into the United States.

Immigration agents monitor and control immigrants residing in the United States. Deportation officers carry out investigations and work with attorneys on matters related to deporting illegal immigrants. Intelligence officers collect and process information. They are aided by research assistants, research specialists, program analysts, and mission support specialists. HSI special agents conduct investigations of suspected illegal activity. Their support staff members include auditors, who are experts in analyzing financial information; criminal research specialists; and investigative assistants. Technical enforcement specialists work with technology such as surveillance systems.

CANADIAN SECURITY INTELLIGENCE SERVICE

The Canadian Security Intelligence Service (CSIS) investigates threats to Canada's national security, analyzes information, and reports to and advises the government of Canada about potential threats. Some of the major areas they handle are terrorism, weapons of mass destruction, spying, foreign interference, and cybersecurity. The CSIS works to both prevent and respond to threats.

Careers at the CSIS encompass the following: technologists who work with science or computer technology, database

INTERVIEW WITH A
TECHNOLOGIST AT CSIS

The following interview is quoted from the CSIS Web site (http://www.csiscareers.ca). Stéphanie's experience is typical of many who work in cybersecurity and other scientific fields related to security.

"I feel like there is a purpose to what I do...that I am doing something for my country," says Stéphanie. After completing a bachelor's degree with a double major in computer science and mathematics, she decided to join the Canadian Security Intelligence Service (CSIS) because she was intrigued by the line of work that intelligence services carry out. Stéphanie has been working as a technologist at the CSIS for six years, and she still finds the work intriguing and stimulating. "When I come into work in the morning, I never know what is in store for me," she says. The dynamic environment in which technologists work presents different challenges and learning opportunities on a daily basis.

While working at the CSIS, she has become knowledgeable in various fields, such as the inner workings of operating systems, network security, protocol analysis, and intrusion detection systems. "In order to be successful in this position, I have had to be open-minded, a quick learner, and able to work as part of a group," Stéphanie explains. Technologists must have a logical mind-set to thoroughly analyze situations, possess the capacity to identify priorities, and display good management skills. In addition, this versatile field also gives employees a chance to travel across Canada and, in some cases, work in cooperation with regional employees. She looks forward to the rest of her career with the CSIS, knowing that, as a technologist, there will always be intriguing challenges and opportunities for growth.

administrators, engineers, scientists, security technologists, programmers, systems analysts, computer system engineers, and computer technicians. Personnel in intelligence (information) collection include intelligence officers, screening analysts, and surveillants (who engage in physical tracking and observation of suspects). Operational, strategic, and tactical analysts evaluate information and make recommendations as to appropriate actions. In addition, the service employs a range of administrative and support personnel in areas such as finance, clerical work, purchasing, public relations, and human resources, among others.

SCIENTIFIC SECURITY

Science plays an important role in security today. The U.S. Department of Homeland Security has two divisions devoted to using science and technology to identify and analyze

A director of the Control Systems Security Program and Industrial Control Systems Cyber Emergency Response Team of the U.S. Department of Homeland Security discusses electrical system security at a cyber security defense lab. Science plays a vital role in modern security, and U.S. agencies employ scientists to examine evidence and to develop new means of detecting and solving crimes.

threats. These are the Information Analysis and Infrastructure Protection Directorate and the Science and Technology Directorate. The Information Analysis and Infrastructure Protection Directorate provides jobs for those with an education in information technology. Positions include security advisers, intelligence operations specialists, IT staff, computer security specialists, and telecommunications specialists. The Science and Technology Directorate employs those with a science degree in biology, computer science, engineering, chemistry, or physics. In addition, most major government security agencies employ individuals with a science background in forensics—the scientific analysis of physical evidence.

chapter 4

PREPARING FOR A CAREER IN SECURITY

To succeed in a security job, one needs people, technical, physical, and general skills. Security today requires more than brute strength. Security professionals must be able to deal with people tactfully. They must have the ability to identify and analyze threats and communicate clearly with superiors and others about them. Further, many security positions require technical expertise to use electronic devices or computers. There are a number of ways a person can prepare himself or herself for a security career while still in high school.

LAYING THE GROUNDWORK

In a security job, a person will be interacting with the public, coworkers, and superiors, and sometimes with representatives of other security organizations. Therefore, people skills and the ability to work as a member of a team are important to have. It is essential to be able to communicate both verbally and in writing because most security jobs involve writing reports and documentation. Therefore, learning English grammar and syntax and how to write clearly are very important. Taking a course in public speaking may be helpful to hone one's ability to communicate verbally.

In the security field, all types of knowledge—mathematical, scientific, psychological, and cultural—are valuable. For this

Today's security professionals are required to recognize and analyze threats using a variety of high-technology systems. Knowledge of both technology and human behavior is valuable on the job.

reason, taking a variety of courses in a broad range of areas is a good idea. These include biology, physics, history, government, English, and math. Anything that helps in understanding what makes things work or understanding people better could turn out to be beneficial later. In addition, for those who are interested in a higher-level position and plan to go to college, such a valuable grounding will make it easier to succeed in their academic career.

Most security jobs today involve using electronic devices, ranging from surveillance cameras to advanced information systems. Therefore, if the school offers a computer course, it's a good idea to take it. Security is an area where extracurricular activities can be important. The more skills an applicant has to offer, the better off he or she will be when the time comes to apply for a job. Because many security jobs are physically demanding, keeping in good shape and developing one's body will be a benefit. Participating in

Many security jobs require personnel to carry and, if necessary, use firearms. Training and practice in using a gun can provide one with the skill to meet firearm requirements.

sports can help a person develop physical strength, dexterity, and stamina. It can also help one learn how to work well as a member of a team. It's not necessary to be a star athlete or make one of the school's major teams. Ordinary intramural or hobby play will work just as well to get a person in shape and keep him or her there. Taking any type of martial arts outside of the school environment is another way to simultaneously achieve good physical condition and develop self-defense skills that may later help one on the job. Technical skills of any sort are also useful in security jobs. Learning how to do photography or practicing using a gun in target shooting, for example, gives one skills that may be helpful when applying or qualifying for a job.

Having a good character and clean criminal record is required in many security positions. Consequently, staying within the law and behaving well are crucial. Any type of security job usually requires a background check showing a clean criminal record, so it is important to stay out of trouble during the teen years.

SECURITY CAREER CERTIFICATION TESTS

Certification is a way of demonstrating mastery of a subject. One organization that offers certification of security professionals is ASIS International (previously the American Society for Industrial Security). ASIS offers three levels of certification: Certified Protection Professional (CPP) for certification in security management, Professional Certified Investigator (PCI), and Physical Security Professional (PSP).

Another organization, NCMS: The Society of Industrial Security Professionals, offers the Industrial Security Professional (ISP) certification. The NCMS certification program is an example of what certification requires. The NCMS certification expects five years of experience working at least part-time in security and passing an exam. The NCMS ISP exam consists of questions in the following areas:

- *Security Administration & Management:* Records, planning, budgeting, staffing, clearances, escorting U.S. citizens without security clearances, and risk management
- *Document Security:* Creating, storing, transmitting, reproducing, destroying, and protecting documents
- *Information Systems Security:* Planning, accreditation, physical protection, controls, forensics, and reporting
- *Physical Security:* Layered protection, locks and security containers, vaults, alarms, closed-circuit TV (CCTV), central alarm stations, access controls and guards, and records
- *Personnel Security:* Forms, clearance, and badges
- *International Security:* Export control regulations; foreign visits and assignments; foreign ownership, control, or influence; and access control

- *Classification:* Identifying critical information, classification system, declassification, and records
- *Security Education:* Requirements and content, ideas and techniques
- *Audits & Self-Assessment:* Audits (examinations of records or facilities)

In addition, applicants must choose two electives in which to answer an additional ten questions each. Electives include intellectual property, COMSEC/TEMPEST (communications security), counterintelligence, operations security, and SAP (systems, applications, and products related to computers).

GAINING EXPERIENCE

Often potential employers in the field value experience that demonstrates high moral character and devotion to duty. For this reason, experiences such as becoming an Eagle Scout in the Boy Scouts, being a member of the Civil Air Patrol, or being a student volunteer with a local law enforcement agency or emergency response or civil defense organization are beneficial. Such activities demonstrate a person's ability to function well in a security environment as well as good character. If it is not possible to get a volunteer position that is directly related to security, volunteer to work at charity or local sporting events. Such work helps to develop general skills working with people and demonstrates good character.

Some government security agencies offer college scholarships to students to help them develop the skills they need. For example, the CIA offers a student scholarship program for high school students planning to attend a four-year college. The program is open to all qualified students, including minority and disabled

A Civil Air Patrol squadron commander addresses cadets. Serving in the Civil Air Patrol can provide one with experience and skills that are desirable to employers in the security field.

students, who perform work related to their major area of interest while attending college. For example, computer science majors work with computers, finance majors in finance, and foreign language majors in translation. Students who are accepted receive a salary, benefits such as health insurance, and a significant amount of college tuition. The NSA offers the Stokes Educational Scholarship Program to high school students, particularly minority high school students, who have demonstrated skills critical to the NSA. The scholarship is open to high school seniors who plan to major in computer science or computer/electrical engineering. Participants attend college during the normal school year and work for the NSA for twelve weeks over the summer. The NSA also offers a work-study program for students learning business or computing skills and a vocational technical (voc-tech) program for students studying graphic arts/printing or manufacturing at voc-tech schools.

chapter 5

EDUCATION FOR A CAREER IN SECURITY

There are a variety of types of training obtainable for those who are interested in a career in security. The type of training required depends heavily on the type of security job that appeals to a person. For some security jobs, employers look for basic mental and physical skills and provide on-the-job training. For others, a college degree is required. For high-level management jobs, cybersecurity, and scientific jobs, an advanced degree may be desirable. Various types of programs and training are available for those interested in a security career.

COLLEGE PROGRAMS

One can approach a security career by earning a degree in criminology, criminal justice, private security, homeland security, cybersecurity, forensics, or another specifically security-related field. This is an area where one can obtain either a two-year (associate's) degree or four-year (bachelor's) degree. Degrees are offered through traditional colleges, community colleges, and technical schools.

A degree course in criminology may include courses in specific types of crime, psychology, government, legal issues and systems, sociology, and logic, among others. Programs in homeland security cover emergency preparedness, security, and counterterrorism. Such programs require courses in political science, psychology, biology, and information technology, as well as specific topics related to emergency planning and response. In addition to degree programs, one can take certificate courses. These programs usually take one year or less and focus on specific skills, such as emergency preparedness. At the end of the course, students receive a certificate indicating that they have mastered the required skills.

The range of jobs in the security field is vast. Some of the highest-paying and most secure positions are those requiring scientific or technological skill. Not all of these jobs require advanced degrees. Scientific research and analysis requires all levels of workers from lab assistants with associate's degrees in biology, chemistry, electronics, or physics to

Understanding the scientific aspects of naturally occurring phenomena such as hurricanes plays an important role in how the Department of Homeland Security predicts and responds to natural disasters.

Ph.D.-level scientists. Similarly, cybersecurity is a subcategory of information technology (IT). Those interested in a degree in IT might consider a specialty in information systems security. An undergraduate or graduate degree in computer science, information technology, or electronics would be of benefit to those considering a career in intelligence gathering or analysis.

Modern security forces require experts in areas such as law and finance. Many security agencies are involved in rooting out fraud and criminal activity related to financial transactions. As a result, those with a degree in a field such as accounting or finance are often of interest to security agencies.

Online courses are another option, which is especially attractive to those who need to obtain a job directly out of high school but wish to further their careers. Online courses are available in areas such as public safety, private security, intelligence analysis, and cybersecurity, among others. Taking such courses and obtaining an online degree, combined with the security experience gained while working in an entry-level job, can improve one's chances of obtaining a promotion or moving on to a better job in another organization. The U.S. Department of Education maintains a database of accredited colleges (http://ope.ed.gov/accreditation) where people can look up colleges by name. If you decide to take online courses, use this database to verify that the institution is accredited and to ensure that you can obtain a valid degree or transfer credits to another school.

NON-COLLEGE CAREER PREPARATION

One does not have to have a college degree to obtain a security job. There are many jobs, such as security guard and TSA security officer, that do not require a degree. These jobs offer a steady salary and good benefits. In addition to benefits such as paid health care, many major corporations offer tuition reimbursement programs. These particular programs pay employees' tuition for college or certificate programs, allowing employees to further their education once they are employed.

Many such jobs have a career path that can lead to a supervisory position with higher pay. The fact that they do not require a degree does not mean that they do not require preparation, however. Many security jobs require applicants to pass various types of written, practical, and physical tests. It is important to have good English and communication skills. Applicants whose first language is not English may be required to take an English test. The flip side of this is that security agencies need personnel who speak languages other than English for positions such as translator and intelligence analyst. If a person is fluent in one or more languages other than English, this ability might be an opportunity for him or her.

Also remember that all major security agencies require support personnel. Although not exotic, a variety of media, clerical, logistical, administrative, equipment operation and maintenance, and other jobs in these agencies can be found on these agencies' Web sites.

Obtaining a certificate specifying mastery of specific skills can help a student obtain a job in the field, if he or she does not plan on attending college. Such stand-alone courses, offered by many colleges, can also help students advance once they have a job.

For students who choose to go into the military after high school, it's worth noting that former military personnel are often in high demand in security jobs. They not only have weapons training but also have developed discipline, maturity, and skill in dealing with difficult situations.

Security is a natural career choice for those who have served in the military. Applicants who have had military experience have already proven their expertise in many of the skills required for security jobs.

SPECIFIC VS. GENERAL EDUCATION FOR SECURITY CAREERS

According to the U.S. Secret Service Web site (http://www.secretservice.gov/kids_faq.shtml), "It's important to study hard in all subjects in school because every day, Secret Service agents use skills from many different areas in their investigations including: science, computer science, law and government, arithmetic, reading comprehension, writing, foreign languages and public speaking." This advice is very informative for anyone interested in any type of security career. Today's crimes are complex and often high tech. The broader one's base of education in high school and college, the better equipped one will be to succeed in a security job and the more skills one will have to offer a potential employer.

One of the most important aspects of succeeding in a security job is the ability to deal with diversity. Security professionals have to deal with not only members of the public who are of various races and cultural backgrounds but also with coworkers and superiors who might come from a variety of backgrounds and ethnicities. In some positions they may be

INTERNSHIPS

An internship is an excellent way to experience firsthand what a security job involves. It can help students decide if the security field is right for them. It can also provide them with practical skills. In addition, internships allow students to develop relationships with professionals in the security field who may later be able to assist them with finding a job or provide a recommendation. A number of security organizations offer internships.

For example, the FBI offers ten-week summer volunteer internships (unpaid) for college students. Students may work at field office locations or the FBI headquarters in Washington, D.C. After students complete the initial internship, additional volunteer internships are available at some offices throughout the year. Although the internships are unpaid, the experience gained can be a benefit when one is applying for a professional security job. The Secret Service also has a student volunteer service that offers college students the opportunity to work at their facilities in Washington, D.C., or at field offices. The Central Intelligence Agency offers both a student internship program and a co-op program whereby students can work in a paid position while they are attending college. The NSA offers a wide variety of internship and summer programs for college students in areas that include computer science, languages, information analysis, and business.

The TSA and ICE both offer paid opportunities for college students. One type of program provides temporary employment for students who want to see if a career in security is right for them. Another type of program provides employment in conjunction with academic programs, allowing students to work in paid positions and sometimes receive academic credit in an area related to their academic area of study. They also offer a number of volunteer positions for students who want to gain experience in the field.

Contact the human resources department of specific agencies to find out what internship opportunities are available. College placement offices may also have information on internship opportunities.

dealing with dignitaries from other countries. They need to be able to deal with people of all backgrounds, races, genders, and ethnicities with tact, diplomacy, and respect. Therefore, taking courses that increase their ability to understand and communicate with those of other cultures, such as history and foreign languages, can be very beneficial.

Key to staying fit for a security career is developing a regular routine of working out to remain in good physical condition. Professionals should be prepared to continue the routine throughout their career.

PHYSICAL FITNESS TRAINING

With the exception of support jobs, such as lab technician, computer information analyst, or clerical positions, most security jobs require a person to be in excellent physical condition. Many private security firms and government security agencies require a minimum level of physical fitness to qualify for a job. Many require applicants to take a physical fitness test to demonstrate that they can meet the physical fitness requirements. For example, the FBI tests applicants who want to be agents on the following:

- The number of sit-ups done in one minute
- A timed 0.19-mile (300-meter) sprint
- The number of push-ups the applicant can do
- A timed 1.5-mile (2.4-kilometer) run

Failing to meet an organization's physical fitness requirements will result in disqualification. Therefore, those interested in a security job should work out, eat right, and develop their physical skills.

chapter 6

Pursuing a Career in Security

Whether one decides to seek a security job directly after high school or go on to college, once one's education is completed, it is necessary to find a job. The information here covers how to get a job in the security field and how to maximize one's chances of success in the field.

Getting a First Job

A good way to get an idea of both the job duties and requirements for the various types of jobs is to check out job ads. The time to do that is several months before graduation from high school or college. Exploring ads will provide insight into what type of job might be available and appealing. Beyond this, it will provide an idea of what courses it is necessary to take or what skills are required to obtain a specific type of job. Examples of sites that provide listings of jobs are Monster (www.monster.com) and Craigslist (www.craigslist.org). These are sites commonly used by companies to post listings for jobs they are trying to fill. The social networking site LinkedIn has become an important source of job postings. LinkedIn is the business version of the personal social networking site Facebook. Companies post ads on these sites, and applicants can respond online. Sites such

Job seekers fill out applications at a job fair. Job fairs are good places to learn about a variety of companies at one time.

as these have become major sources for companies to fill jobs, and they should play a role in any job search. There are a number of other ways to locate potential jobs.

Those who attend college should contact the institution's placement office, which can help students find jobs. Often job fairs are held at colleges or at the community level. Companies send representatives to these fairs to talk to applicants about the company and jobs available. Because most companies require security staff, practically any company representative could be worth talking to about possible openings in the field. Agencies of the U.S. government post job listings online, as do many major corporations. So check out their Web sites. There is usually a link labeled "Jobs," or something similar, where applicants can check out openings.

Networking is an excellent way to find out about jobs. Talk to people you or your family know who work at companies that may need security staff. Find out whom to talk to at the company about a possible job. It is also possible to contact the security manager at a corporation and tell that person you are a student and would like to learn about security jobs. Often managers are willing to talk to students, and they may know people you could contact about possible work.

The least effective way to find a job is usually to rely on want ads in the newspaper. By all means, respond to an ad if one is appealing. However, huge numbers of people respond to every want ad, and the majority of jobs available never make it to the want ad stage. Many are filled by word of mouth or posted electronically instead. Because most jobs are not advertised, it is often more effective to send a résumé directly to companies one is interested in working for. They may have job openings that are not advertised or positions may open up in the future. Send a résumé to the director of security or human resources. Applicants should include a brief cover letter explaining the type of job they are interested in, briefly noting why they think their education and experience would make them a benefit to the company. There are many books available on writing résumés and cover letters. The want ad section of the newspaper can be used to identify companies in a particular geographic area. One can also use resources such as Standard & Poor's directory of companies. This directory should be available at the local library and provides details about thousands of companies.

The most important element in obtaining job interviews is persistence. It may be necessary to send out a large number of résumés and to keep sending more out each week until one gets a job.

PREPARING A RÉSUMÉ

The most important tool for job hunting is a résumé (a document that lists part-time or internship job experience, educational background, and other information about the applicant). The purpose of a résumé is to get an interview with prospective employers. Therefore, it should include information that shows that the applicant has skills in areas that will make him or her valuable and successful in that job and company. Here are some tips for composing a successful résumé.

Applicants should use a format that makes it easy to tell what type of job they are interested in and what their past experience is. Think about the company's industry and the specific job being applied for. Applicants should include nontechnical skills that would make them successful in the field. Don't include a lot of irrelevant personal information, but do include personal information when it is relevant, such as foreign languages and martial arts training, or participation on a sports team, which demonstrates physical fitness. Those who have donated time to charitable organizations should mention that. Companies are increasingly interested in playing a meaningful

Tomas Alvarez
143 Main Street
Worcester, Massachusetts 01601
Home: (508) 624-9973/Cell: (508) 624-7389
talvarez@isp.net

Objective: To obtain a position as a security manager where I can use my experience and expertise to implement and manage security programs to keep the company's premises safe for visitors and employees.

Professional Experience

Consolidated Widget Corporation, Bellevue, MA 2011–Present
Security Supervisor

Supervised 15 security guards.

Planned assignments and oversaw scheduling of security guards to ensure that all areas of company premises were secure.

Created plan for regular testing and maintenance of security systems, including CCTV, security cameras, and alarm systems.

Provided timely reports to corporate management.

Implemented procedures for checking in and escorting visitors to the company.

Researched and recommended improved systems and updates to existing systems to keep company secure in face of evolving threats.

Assisted security manager in conducting research for annual risk analysis of potential threats to company and planning for emergency response.

International Construction Materials Corporation, Worcester, MA 2008–2010
Security Guard

Responsible for patrolling warehouse containing several million dollars' worth of construction materials to maintain security.

Used sophisticated electronic equipment, including CCTV and key card systems, to ensure security of premises.

Prepared daily, weekly, and monthly reports for supervisor.

Made recommendations for improvements to security systems to improve security of warehouse.

Education

Worcester Technical High School, 2008
Associate's degree, 2010, Institute of Technology, Security Systems
Bachelor's degree, 2012, University of Massachusetts, Criminal Justice
Firearms certification

Additional Skills

Black belt in karate
Fluent in Spanish
Volunteer Massachusetts Civil Air Patrol

References available on request

This example of a résumé for a position in the security field highlights experience at different levels, including both introductory and supervisory positions.

role in their communities, and volunteering shows that an applicant is the kind of person who is willing to help others, not just himself or herself.

Above all, applicants should make sure that their résumé is neat, professional looking, and thoroughly proofread so that it does not contain mistakes. No company wants to hire a sloppy security professional.

THE INTERVIEW

The purpose of a résumé is to get an interview. It is in the interview that an applicant convinces a prospective employer to hire him or her. Applicants' personal presentation will have a significant impact. They should dress in business-appropriate clothing and be well groomed. They should speak respectfully, answer questions calmly, and use correct grammar. If asked about experience or skills they don't have, applicants should explain why their education or background equips them to learn those skills. Sometimes interviewers ask questions designed to see how applicants react under stress or analyze problems. Realize that how one responds to such questions, not the solution one provides, is what they want to see. Applicants need to show that they can break the problem down and consider what would be

The interview provides the opportunity to demonstrate professionalism and people skills as well as discuss specific security training and experience.

possible to do. Often more than one person will interview an applicant. Applicants should be sure to treat everyone they meet politely. The lead interviewer will be evaluating applicants' people skills as well as their answers to questions.

TIPS FOR THE SECURITY JOB INTERVIEW

The following tips are adapted from "10 Do's and Don'ts for Security Job Interviews," by Joan Goodchild, senior editor of *CSO Magazine:*

- *Be sure your résumé is perfect:* An outstanding résumé is necessary to even get an interview.
- *Do research the company:* An understanding of the company and its history can impress an interviewer.
- *Don't forget to prepare:* Find out about the company so that you can show you understand its problems.
- *Do practice answering tough questions in advance:* Write out the answers to questions such as "Tell me about yourself," and "What are your weaknesses?" and practice them so that you can answer fluently when asked.
- *Don't emphasize your "cops and robbers" background:* Don't emphasize your "tough-guy" side; instead present yourself as a professional.
- *Show them you are a [professional] who understands security:* Show you understand the management side of security, such as the need to be cost-efficient and why specific things need to be done.
- *Don't get caught up in past accomplishments:* Emphasize what you can do for the company in the future, not what you've done in the past.
- *Do provide examples of how you would solve problems:* Give a concrete example of how you approach a problem the company might face.
- *Don't forget to follow up:* Send a written thank-you note.
- *Do take the right tone in your follow-up:* Be pleasant, appreciative, and understanding, not demanding.

BEING PROFESSIONAL

In security, one is dealing with members of the public and sometimes dignitaries. It is important that security personnel's dress, attitude, and behavior are professional. Some security jobs require security professionals to wear a uniform. If so, it should always be clean and unwrinkled. Those who work in street clothes should ensure that their clothing is appropriate for a professional: a suit or slacks, shirt, and tie for men and a suit, business-appropriate dress, or slacks suit for women. One's shoes should be polished and one's hair cut. It is not appropriate to wear piercings or loud makeup or jewelry.

Security professionals should always treat members of the public with respect, even when it is necessary to enforce rules, and they must deal tactfully with people of different genders, races, and ethnicities. If security personnel dress and act like professionals, the people they deal and work with are more likely to treat them as professionals. In addition, management is more likely to promote people whom they see as professional and probably think of them as capable of controlling themselves in challenging situations.

glossary

aftermath The effects that follow a disaster or event.

asylum Refuge granted to person from another country.

audit To examine records or facilities.

bail Money put up by a person accused of a crime to ensure the person shows up for his or her court date.

bail bondsman A person who lends bail money to people accused of crimes.

bounty Money paid for the return of a fugitive.

clandestine Hidden or secret.

congregate Gather together.

contract labor Workers hired on an as-needed basis.

co-op program A cooperative education program whereby classroom-based education is combined with practical work experience.

copyright The exclusive right to a written or artistic work.

corruption Engaging in dishonest activities or convincing another person to do so.

counterfeiting Making fake money or goods.

counterterrorism The stopping of terrorists.

crime prevention The placement of safeguards to prevent crimes.

cybersecurity Protection of data and computer systems.

deport To send a person back to the country from which he or she came.

dexterity Skill in manipulating objects with one's hands.

digital Stored in electronic format.

dignitary Very important person (VIP).

disaster management Responding to damaging natural or man-made events.

drug trafficking Transporting and distributing illegal or controlled substances.

emergency preparedness Advance planning for responding to a natural disaster, terrorist attack, or other catastrophic event.

evacuate To remove people from an area where there is danger.

felony A serious crime.

first responder A person charged with being first on the scene in the event of a crime or disaster.

forensics The scientific analysis of physical evidence.

fraud Cheating a person out of money or items of value.

freelance A self-employed person who works for clients on an as-needed basis.

hacker A person who breaks into others' computer systems.

illegal alien An immigrant who has entered a country without permission.

industrial espionage Stealing company secrets.

infrastructure The facilities and systems required to run a city, state, or country, such as communication systems, highways, and utilities.

integrity The physical soundness of a structure.

intellectual property An idea, invention, or process that originates from the work of the mind or intellect. Traditional intellectual property rights include copyrights, patents, and trademarks, and unlike tangible property, these are not eliminated when the property is destroyed.

intelligence analyst Person who evaluates information about possible threats.

liable Legally responsible for.

logistics The process of moving supplies to where they are needed.

loss prevention Protection from theft.

on call Expected to report to work or deal with problems on an as-needed basis when off-duty.

patent The exclusive right to manufacture, sell, or license an invention.

personal security Protecting a person's life and body; bodyguard services.

physical security The protection of property from damage.

private sector Businesses and organizations under private, rather than government, control.

prohibited Forbidden.

prospective Potential.

public sector Organizations, institutions, and agencies under government control.

sabotage To deliberately destroy, damage, or obstruct something.

social networking Online resources that connect people with each other to share personal information.

specifications Detailed technical requirements.

stamina Endurance; the ability to engage in physical activity for an extended period.

surveillant Person who follows a suspect to observe his or her destination or activities.

treacherous Dangerous or unsafe.

vandalism The willful destruction of property.

venue Location or facility.

virtual Existing in electronic format on a computer.

white-collar crime Nonviolent crimes committed by businesspeople, often of a financial nature.

for more information

ASIS International
Worldwide Headquarters
1625 Prince Street
Alexandria, VA 22314-2818
(703) 519-6200
Web site: http://www.asisonline.org
This organization provides publications, news, job information, certifications, and other resources for security
industry professionals.

Canadian Security Association (CANASA)
National Headquarters
50 Acadia Avenue, Suite 201
Markham, ON L3R 0B3
Canada
(905) 513-0622
Toll-free in Canada: (800) 538-9919
Web site: http://www.canasa.org
CANASA is a national not-for-profit organization dedicated to
advancing the security industry and supporting security
professionals in Canada.

Canadian Security Intelligence Service
1941 Ogilvie Road
Ottawa, ON K1J 1B7
Canada
(613) 993-9620
Web site: http://www.csis.gc.ca
This organization is responsible for operations designed to
protect the security of Canada. Its Web site includes
information on jobs.

Central Intelligence Agency (CIA)
Office of Public Affairs
Washington, DC 20505
(703) 482-0623
Web site: http://www.cia.gov
This organization is responsible for activities outside the
    United States related to U.S. national security. Its Web
    site has information on jobs and student programs.

Federal Bureau of Investigation (FBI)
FBI Headquarters
935 Pennsylvania Avenue NW
Washington, DC 20535-0001
(202) 324-3000
Web site: http://www.fbi.gov
This agency of the U.S. government is responsible for the
    protection of U.S. financial institutions and investigating
    major crimes. Its Web site contains information on jobs
    and student programs.

National Security Agency
9800 Savage Road
Fort Meade, MD 20755
(301) 688-6524
Web site: http://www.nsa.gov
This agency of the U.S. government is responsible for collect-
    ing and analyzing information to protect the United
    States. Its Web site includes information on jobs and
    student programs.

NCMS: The Society of Industrial Security Professionals
National Headquarters
994 Old Eagle School Road, Suite 1019

Wayne, PA 19087-1866

(610) 971-4856

Web site: https://www.classmgmt.com

This society of industrial security professionals offers
publications, a scholarship program, and an industrial
security professional certification program.

U.S. Bureau of Labor Statistics (BLS)

Division of Information and Marketing Services

2 Massachusetts Avenue NE, Room 2850

Washington, DC 20212

(202) 691-5200

Web site: http://www.bls.gov

This bureau provides guides to and statistics on careers in
various industries.

U.S. Department of Homeland Security (DHS)

Washington, DC 20528

(202) 282-8000

Web site: http://www.dhs.gov

This U.S. government department is responsible for coor-
dination of activities related to protecting the United
States. Its Web site includes information on jobs and
resources on homeland security.

U.S. Immigration and Customs Enforcement

500 12th Street SW

Washington, DC 20536

(866) 347-2423

Web site: http://www.ice.gov

An agency of the U.S. government, this department is
responsible for controlling the flow of people and goods
across U.S. borders. Its Web site contains information
on jobs and student programs.

U.S. Secret Service
245 Murray Drive, Building 410
Washington, DC 20223
(202) 406-5830
Web site: http://www.secretservice.gov
This U.S. government agency is responsible for the protection
    of U.S. and foreign dignitaries and government sites. Its
    Web site includes information on jobs and student
    programs.

WEB SITES

Due to the changing nature of Internet links, Rosen Publishing
has developed an online list of Web sites related to the subject
of this book. This site is updated regularly. Please use this link
to access the list:

http://www.rosenlinks.com/ECAR/Secu

for further reading

Ackerman, Thomas H. *FBI Careers: The Ultimate Guide to Landing a Job as One of America's Finest.* Indianapolis, IN: JIST, 2009.

Blackwell, Amy Hackney. *Career Launcher: Law Enforcement and Public Safety.* New York, NY: Ferguson Publishing, 2011.

Bolles, Richard. *What Color Is Your Parachute?: A Practical Manual for Job-Hunters and Job-Changers.* New York, NY: Crown/Random House, 2013.

Brezina, Corona. *Careers in Law Enforcement.* New York, NY: Rosen Publishing, 2009.

Brezina, Corona. *Public Security in an Age of Terrorism.* New York, NY: Rosen Publishing, 2009.

Camenson, Blythe. *Opportunities in Forensic Science.* New York, NY: McGraw-Hill, 2009.

Echaore-McDavid, Susan. *Career Opportunities in Forensic Science.* New York, NY: Checkmark Books, 2008.

Fry, Ron. *101 Great Answers to the Toughest Interview Questions.* Boston, MA: Course Technology, 2009.

Hanson, Paul. *Operations Officer and Careers in the CIA.* Berkeley Heights, NJ: Enslow Publishing, 2007.

Harmon, Daniel E. *Careers in Internet Security.* New York, NY: Rosen Publishing, 2011.

Harr, J. Scott, and Karen M. Hess. *Careers in Criminal Justice and Related Fields: From Internship to Promotion.* Belmont, CA: Wadsworth Publishing, 2009.

Holcomb, Raymond. *Endless Enemies: Inside FBI Counterterrorism.* Dulles, VA: Potomac Books, 2011.

Karlitz, Gail. *Virtual Apprentice: FBI Agent.* New York, NY: Ferguson Publishing, 2009.

Kennedy, Joyce Lain. *Cover Letters for Dummies.* Hoboken, NJ: Wiley Publishing, 2009.

Kennedy, Joyce Lain. *Job Interviews for Dummies.* Hoboken, NJ: Wiley Publishing, 2011.

Kennedy, Joyce Lain. *Résumés for Dummies.* Hoboken, NJ: Wiley Publishing, 2011.

Mayer, Jared. *Extreme Careers: Homeland Security Officers.* New York, NY: Rosen Publishing, 2007.

Porterfield, Jason. *Careers as a Cyberterrorism Expert.* New York, NY: Rosen Publishing, 2011.

Taylor, Karol, and Janet Ruck. *Guide to America's Federal Jobs: A Complete Directory of U.S. Government Career Opportunities.* Indianapolis, IN: JIST, 2009.

Troutman, Kathryn Kraemer. *Federal Résumé Guide: Strategies for Writing a Winning Federal Résumé.* 5th ed. Indianapolis, IN: JIST, 2011.

Watson, Stephanie. *A Career as a Police Officer.* New York, NY: Rosen Publishing, 2011.

Whiteman, Lily Madeleine. *How to Land a Top-Paying Federal Job: Your Complete Guide to Opportunities, Internships, Résumés and Cover Letters, Networking, Interviews, Salaries, Promotions, and More!* New York, NY: AMACOM, 2012.

bibliography

Central Intelligence Agency. "Career Opportunities."
Retrieved July 26, 2012 (https://www.cia.gov/careers/
opportunities/index.html).

Eastern Michigan University. "Curriculum in Criminology
and Criminal Justice." Retrieved August 8, 2012
(http://catalog.emich.edu/preview_program.php?catoid=
1&poid=362).

Federal Bureau of Investigation. "Quick Facts." Retrieved July
26, 2012 (http://www.fbi.gov/about-us/quick-facts).

Goodchild, Joan. "10 Do's and Don'ts for Security Job
Interviews." *CSO*. Retrieved August 28, 2012 (http://
www.csoonline.com/article/490926/10-dos-and-don-ts
-for-security-job-interviews?page=3).

Immigration and Customs Enforcement. "Careers." Retrieved
August 5, 2012 (http://www.ice.gov/careers).

"Maria" (TSA security officer). Interview with the author,
August 25, 2012.

National Security Agency. "Careers." Retrieved July 26, 2012
(http://www.nsa.gov/careers/index.shtml).

NCMS ISP. "Industrial Security Professional (ISP)
Certification Program Requirements and Application."
February 2012. Retrieved August 26, 2012 (http://www
.ncms-isp.org/documents/brochure.pdf).

Neyman, Julia. "Colleges Embrace Homeland Security
Curriculum." *USA Today*, August 24, 2004. Retrieved
(http://www.usatoday.com/news/education/2004-08-24
-homeland-usat_x.htm).

Secret Service. *Secret Service Strategic Plan 2006–2013*.
Retrieved July 23, 2012 (http://www.secretservice.gov/
usss_strategic_plan_2008_2013.pdf).

Strom, Kevin, et al. *The Private Security Industry: A Review of Definitions: Available Data Sources, and Paths Moving Forward.* Research Triangle Park, NC: RTI International/Bureau of Justice Statistics, 2009.

Transportation Security Administration. "Join Us." Retrieved August 5, 2012 (http://www.tsa.gov/join/index.shtm).

University of Maryland University College. "Major in Homeland Security." Retrieved August 8, 2012 (http://www.umuc.edu/undergrad/ugprograms/hmls.cfm).

Walker, Cathy. "Four Tips: How to Land an IT Security Job." *InformationWeek*, April 9, 2012. Retrieved August 28, 2012 (http://www.informationweek.com/global-cio/careers/4-tips-how-to-land-an-it-security-job/232800473).

Watson, Joe. *Where the Jobs Are Now.* New York, NY: McGraw-Hill, 2010.

index

A

ASIS International, 44
associate's degrees, 48, 49

B

background checks, 22, 24, 32, 43
benefits, 7, 8, 13, 25, 47, 51
bodyguards, 24, 25
bounty hunters, 23
Boy Scouts, 45

C

Canadian Security Intelligence
    Service (CSIS), 35–37
    interview with a technologist, 36
Central Intelligence Agency (CIA),
    30, 45 47, 54
Certified Protection Professional
    (CPP), 44
Civil Air Patrol, 45
college, 5, 17, 28, 38, 41, 45–47,
    51, 55, 57, 59
    courses to take for a security job,
    48–50, 53, 54
corporate security, 14–16
counterterrorism, 6, 7
crime prevention and investigation,
    6, 7
criminology degree, 48
cybersecurity, 6, 7, 9, 17–20, 28, 35,
    48, 50

D

danger, and a career in security, 13,
    14, 19, 20, 25, 28
Department of Homeland Security
    (DHS), 12, 26, 31, 33, 37
disaster management, 6, 7

E

emergency preparedness, 6, 7
Enforcement and Removal
    Operations, 33
extracurricular activities, as preparation
    for security career, 41–43, 45

F

Federal Bureau of Investigation
    (FBI), 28–30, 54, 56
first responders, 7, 19
foreign languages, 31, 51, 53
forensic technology, 9, 38

H

homeland security degree, 49
Homeland Security Investigations
    (HSI), 33, 35
hours and schedule, 8

I

immigration enforcement, 12, 13,
    33–35
Industrial Security Professional
    (ISP), 44–45

ABOUT THE AUTHOR

Jeri Freedman has a B.A. from Harvard University. She is the author of numerous nonfiction books, including *Career Building Through Skinning and Modding, Careers in Emergency Medical Response Teams, Search and Rescue, Careers in Computer Science and Programming, Women in the Workplace: Wages, Respect, and Equal Rights, Careers in Pharmaceutical Sales,* and *Dream Jobs in the Sports Industry.*

PHOTO CREDITS

Designer: Matt Cauli; Editor: Kathy Kuhtz Campbell; Photo Researcher: Karen Huang